what's your excuse
for not loving
your job

What's Your Excuse for not Loving Your Job?

This first edition published in 2016 by WYE Publishing
9 Evelyn Gardens, Richmond TW9 2PL
www.wyepublishing.com

ISBN 978-0-9933388-6-1

Cover and text design by Annette Peppis & Associates

Printed in UK by Lightning Source

www.whatsyourexcuse.co.uk
Follow What's Your Excuse…? on Twitter – @whats_yr_excuse
https://www.facebook.com/whatsyourexcusebooks

http://coachingwithamanda.com
Follow Amanda on Twitter – @AmandaCcoach

Contents

Introduction

How to use this book

You have a job. It may be a good job, it could even be a great job, but something is missing, and that something is love. You don't **love** your job.

This book will help you change that. It offers lots of practical ideas for tackling the things which may be making you unhappy at work, and it will help you to find your own way to love your job.

How often do you hear someone say they love their job? Occasionally you will. Maybe you've even said it yourself at some point in the past, but you're not saying it now.

This is pretty sad. We spend a lot of time at work so we owe it to ourselves to spend that time doing something we love. If you think this is unrealistic, think again.

As I was writing this book, I was primarily writing for those of you who are employed by an organisation, whether large or small. Most of the time I also pictured someone who has a boss, and who might or might not have a team reporting to them. However if you are self-employed or if you are very senior you will still find useful hints and tips here.

I've worked in a large corporation and I've been self-employed. There have been times when I loved my job and I felt really lucky to have a job which I enjoyed and which I was good at. The days flew by and I never resented the time I spent at work. There have also been times when I hated my job. I found it tedious and value-less. I felt compromised, doing a job I didn't believe in just because I was too scared to make changes. It took me far too long to make those changes.

I don't want anyone else to spend years in a job they don't love, when a few simple actions may be all that's needed to transform the situation. So this book looks at all those excuses we make when we're not happy in our work, but haven't yet found the motivation to do some-thing about it. This book will give you that motivation.

It doesn't mean you'll have to change jobs (though that may be one option). It does mean you have to be prepared to look at your job differently, and to take some action.

I have grouped excuses into categories. Sometimes the same issue can show up in more than one way, so you may find the same course of action suggested in more than one place – where this is the case I will also point you to other related excuses and advice.

It's up to you how you use this book. Maybe you know the reason you don't love your job, and you can therefore jump straight to the relevant section. Or per-haps you know there's something not quite right, but you aren't sure what. In that case you may want to skim quickly through the whole book until a particular excuse or section grabs your attention. Then you can focus in and explore some more.

And if your favourite excuse isn't here in this book, please do let me know. I'd love to include it in a future edition.

The benefits of loving your job

Before you start reading the excuses, it's a good idea to get clear on why you want to address how you feel about your job. So grab a pen and paper, your smart phone or your tablet, and just jot down what you think will improve when you feel happier in your work.

Here are some ideas to get you started:
- I will be nicer to live with at home
- I won't be resentful and grumpy with my friends
- I will have more energy and enthusiasm
- I won't feel that time at work is time wasted
- I will feel that I am achieving something
- I will be able to hold my head up when I'm talking about my job
- I will enjoy weekends and holidays without dreading the return to work
- I will be more confident
- I won't envy other people who love what they do
- I will be making the most of every day
- I won't feel that life is passing me by

Now add some of your own.

The consequences of not loving your job

In case you need further reasons to take action, here are some of the downsides of having a job you don't love:

- You won't do your best and that could make you feel guilty
- You will feel frustrated and stuck
- You will be tired and have less energy
- You will find yourself thinking and worrying about work even at the weekend
- You will find it harder to switch off when you go on holiday
- You won't be fulfilling your potential
- You may look back in later years and regret those missed opportunities
- You will resent your friends who enjoy their jobs more than you do
- Your health may suffer
- You won't be a good role model for your children
- You will be miserable both inside work *and* outside it

Again, feel free to come up with your own ideas.

A word of warning before you read further

I set out to write this book to help people who have a job that isn't quite satisfying enough and where a few changes could make all the difference.

For some of us, however, not enjoying our work is a sign that there are more serious issues to address. This book is not intended to be a replacement for counselling or therapy. So if as you read this book you realise that you have a more deep-rooted issue – perhaps you are depressed or maybe you are being harassed at work – please seek appropriate help.

This may be your GP or it could be the HR department at your place of work, or you could start with talking to your partner, parent or a close friend.

Taking some action will be the first step to improving things.

The Excuses

The Work

I don't like the work

It will help if you can spend some time identifying exactly what it is you don't like. And then take a look at the most relevant excuse below.

But also ask yourself if this is a temporary or new feeling - do you usually like the work? If so, what has changed? Have you gained a new responsibility or taken on a different role? Remember that it can take time to get comfortable with something new, so give it a chance.

It can take time to get comfortable with something new

If this is a new feeling, set yourself a timescale to really give it your all. Three months is often a good period – long enough to allow yourself to get used to changes but not so long it feels like there is no end in sight. Tell yourself that for those three months, you will be fully committed in two ways:

- To do the best job you can
- To find a way to love your work

The first commitment speaks for itself. The second may require more thought. One approach is a technique called 'look for the 2%'. If you loved just 2% of the work you do, what would that element be? What is it about that 2% that you love? If this isn't immediately obvious, take time over the next few days at work to notice when you are most engaged. Typically this will be when time passes quickly and you suddenly realise that an hour, or half a day, has passed and it is coffee time, lunchtime or time to go home!

What were you doing that engaged you? And what about it was engaging? For example, maybe you were tackling a chunky problem. Was it the analysis or the problem solving that you enjoyed? Or was it the opportunity to really focus in on detail – or the chance to brainstorm solutions with colleagues?

Once you are clear on the activity that you enjoy, ask yourself how you can bring more of that into your work. Maybe you have sufficient control over your work to do this yourself. If not, you may have to ask a more senior colleague to help you find opportunities to spend more time on this kind of activity.

Challenge yourself to keep increasing the percentage of the work you enjoy. Can you shift it from 2% to 10%, then to 30% and then to 50%? At what point will you realise that you now love enough of your work to say 'I love my job'?

I have too much work

There can be a number of reasons for having too much work, but they will all fall into one of these two categories:

- The organisation's overall workload is high and there aren't enough people to do it
- Your natural tendency is to accept everything that comes your way without stopping to consider whether you have the capacity to do it

How you tackle this issue depends on the underlying cause.

If the issue is excess work throughout the organisation, then your challenge is to reduce the workload in one of the following ways:

- Increase resource
- Reduce work
- Streamline activity

If you are senior in the organisation then increasing resource may be a viable option, because you may have the authority and/or influence to facilitate this. Get clear on the business case for additional resource: what will the organisation be able to do better as a result?

Even if your role is not senior you may be able to influence others to consider hiring additional resource. Again your starting point should be to identify the benefit to the organisation of more resource.

These could be benefits such as faster turnaround of work, higher quality work, more cost effective processes (by bringing in more junior staff to support those with greater experience and expertise) or fewer HR issues such as stress, other illness and absenteeism.

To reduce work, the key question is, 'what can we stop doing?' Is there something that the organisation as a whole does or that you as an individual do which has no value? If so, why are you doing it? What would be the consequence of not doing it? Try stopping this activity for a short time to see whether there is any adverse impact.

To streamline activity, you need to think about how things could be done more efficiently. This comes naturally to some people and not to others. So if it isn't one of your strengths don't be ashamed or embarrassed to ask for help. Maybe there is a colleague who is always super organised and who would be flat-tered and delighted to share their techniques. Or do you have a friend outside work who is the king or queen of organisation? You may not be able to share with them

Don't be ashamed or embarrassed to ask for help

the detail of your work (for confidentiality reasons) but you can almost certainly share the types of activity that bog you down and make you inefficient.

Or make a game of it. Get your team together and brainstorm as many ways as you can of streamlining things. The rule when brainstorming is that anything is possible and permissible, however whacky or apparently impractical. So challenge yourselves to come up with 50 things you could do differently– or 100! Write them all down – perhaps on a flipchart or large sheet of paper so you can all see them. Take a coffee/tea break and then come back and explore which of these suggestions has a grain of possibility and practicality. You'll be surprised how sometimes the most 'off the wall' suggestion can trigger a realistic solution.

If, on the other hand, this is not an issue of excess work for the organisation, but of you taking on work without the capacity to do it, you may need to adopt a different approach. Check out *"Everyone delegates to me"* in the section covering your colleagues.

I don't have enough work

Now some people might dream of a time when they could say this! Maybe you have done so in the past.

But the reality is that when we don't have enough work most of us hate it. It's often really boring. Time drags and we end up feeling guilty because we put off the jobs we do have, as there is no incentive to get them done.

If it's a short-term issue (maybe you know it's your quiet season, or a big project is just about to launch) then make the most of the opportunity to have a clear-out - physical, technological and mental.

Make the most of the opportunity to have a clear-out

Your physical clear-out will involve going through papers, files, drawers etc. and being ruthless about throwing out anything you don't need. Also take a look at your workspace and check whether there is anything that could be refreshed – pictures or notices on the walls, photos or ornaments on the desk, etc.

Your technological clear-out involves getting rid of anything that is unnecessarily cluttering up your computer or smart phone – multiple earlier versions of documents, for example, or unimportant emails that haven't been deleted. It's also critical to make sure that you have saved anything of importance to somewhere where it can readily be retrieved if your technology plays up. In most larger organisations this will be taken care of for you but it won't hurt to check. If you work in a small organisation or are self-employed it's probably up to you to back up your work and make sure you can access important emails from elsewhere if necessary.

Your mental clear-out is the one that many people neglect. It's about taking stock of what has happened at work over the previous months, both positive and negative. Look at what you have achieved, ask yourself what you are proud of and give yourself a pat on the back. Look at where things went wrong, ask yourself what could have gone better and consider what you have learned from the experience. Then look forward to the next few months. Ask yourself what you want to continue doing, what you want to stop doing, and what you'd like to do differently.

If lack of work is a long-term issue, then you have three options:

* Accept it and find other ways to occupy yourself when you're not busy
* Ask the boss for more or different work, explaining that you are capable of doing more
* Start looking for another job that will be more satisfying

It's up to you to decide which of these approaches is best for you at this stage in your working life.

I hate all the admin

A certain amount of admin forms part of any job – in fact part of pretty well everything we do – and it's what makes things run smoothly. Many of us find there are some pieces of admin we are happy to do, and others that drive us mad!

The key is to work out how to deal with the admin efficiently, and to streamline the bits you don't enjoy as much as possible. You probably do this already in some aspects of daily life – paying utility bills by direct debit, for example.

I suggest you start by making a list of all the admin jobs that crop up frequently in your work. Then divide them into three lists:

1   The ones you are happy to do
2   The (remaining) ones that you must do yourself
3   The ones you could delegate to someone else, do less frequently, or stop doing without serious consequences.

Each of these lists needs different treatment and I'm going to tackle them in reverse order.

To get results quickly, start focusing on the third list. Quick results will motivate you to tackle the other lists.

List 3 needs to be further divided into Delegate,

Reduce, Stop. The 'Stop' list speaks for itself. Just don't do these admin tasks anymore!

Look at the 'Reduce' list and decide how often these tasks really need to be tackled, then schedule slots in your diary to deal with them. You may want to group some of them together for an occasional admin blitz, or this may fill you with horror, in which case space them out.

Review the 'Delegate' list now and work out who should take on each task. Then tell them, clearly, politely and firmly. Don't be afraid to consider delegating upwards. Sometimes a more senior colleague is able to deal with things more quickly or effectively than you can.

Once you have dealt with List 3, you can turn your attention to List 2.

Don't be afraid to consider delegating upwards

First of all, just check in with yourself and make sure you *really* have to deal with everything on this list yourself. Quite sure? If not, then delegate them too.

Look at the remaining tasks. Is there a way you can do them more efficiently? Perhaps you could use technology to support you better, or you could group together the activities that require data from the same source, or a similar approach, or addressing with the same frequency. Do you need more training to deal with this admin more efficiently? If so where can you get it? Take action now to organise or ask for it.

Now you have worked out how to tackle these tasks, you need to turn to your diary again and schedule them just as you did with List 3.

Finally, it's time to consider List 1. You may be happy to do these tasks, but it's still a good idea to reassess how you do them. Even with these, use the 'Delegate, Reduce or Stop' approach to identify whether you are tackling them correctly, think about whether there is a better way to do them, and get them in your diary so you do them only when they need doing.

I'm in a dead end job

If you enjoy your job but there is no prospect of it leading to anything bigger, then make the most of it for now and be clear that there will come a time when you need to move on.

> Grab every opportunity you can to develop skills

For now, grab every opportunity you can to develop skills that will make you more marketable in the future. If you are offered training by your employer, take it. If not, look at other ways to add new skills, perhaps by doing an evening class, volunteering with a local charity or other organisation, or by finding a mentor you admire and asking them to talk to you about their work.

The Organisation

The work we do is meaningless

There are lots of people who think their work is meaningless and there are some fabulous stories of people in humble jobs who really see meaning and value in what they do. For example, a cleaner at a pool where Paralympic swimmers train said his job was to get a gold medal.

What is the value that you can find in your job? This might not be about the purpose of your organisation; it could be about how you contribute to making your team better, how you make life more enjoyable for those around you or how the work you do enables your family to have a better life, because of the money that you bring in.

You may also want to read *"Nobody values the work I do"* under Recognition later in this book.

The organisation isn't successful

It's not much fun working for an organisation that is struggling, and much more fun and exciting to be working in an organisation that is growing and vibrant. However, before you write the organisation off as a disaster or decide to change jobs make sure you are clear on whether the organisation is going through a temporary bad patch, or whether it really is on the slippery slope to failure.

What incentive do you need to give it 100% effort?

Also be clear on how much you can personally do to turn the organisation into a success. If you could contribute to making it more successful then what incentive do you need to give it 100% effort? All too often people think that the only incentive is money but it isn't. Your incentive could be valuable experience to stand you in good stead in your career, or it could be a desire to protect the jobs of those with whom you work, or it could be that you really believe in the product or service offered by your organisation and that you would really love to make sure this product or service is out there in the marketplace.

So dig deep and see whether you can find your motivation to make the required effort. If you can, then go for it. Give yourself a timeframe and recognise that if by the end of this time you have not made a difference it will be time to move on.

I don't believe in the organisation

What is it that you don't believe in? Is it that you don't believe in the organisation's purpose and objectives? Or is it that you don't believe the organisation can be successful?

If you don't believe in the organisation's purpose can you find something that matters to you - perhaps helping colleagues? If you don't believe that the organisation can be successful, what can you contribute to improve its chances?

Decide whether this is something worth doing and if so embrace it wholeheartedly and give it your full commitment. If not, then this may be the time to start looking for another job.

I don't understand what we're trying to do

Is there a communication issue here? Of course it would be good if your management explained the organisation's objectives clearly but that doesn't always happen; so it's your responsibility to ask questions that will help you understand. Communication is a two way process.

You could start by checking in with your colleagues whether they understand what you're trying to do. If they do, then great! They can explain it to you. If not then you have a stronger reason to ask people above you in the organisation to explain.

Maybe you could brainstorm with your colleagues what the key questions are and get really clear on this so that you command the respect of your management by not wasting their time with waffle. Then consider the best time and method to ask your question. Avoid email if at all possible, as it is not the most effective communication method.

A little of this preparation on your part will show your management that you care about the questions you're asking.

I don't like what the organisation stands for

This is an issue relating to values, ie. what's most important to you. What you're saying is that your values are not aligned with those of the organisation. This is a tricky one; you may have to decide the extent to which you are prepared to compromise your values. If the compromise is too great then you need to either change the organisation or change jobs.

Before you decide to take the drastic step of changing jobs think about how you might help the company to change. The bigger the organisation the longer it will take to change. Remember the analogy that it takes a long time to turn a steamship around but much less time to turn small motorboat around. Nonetheless it is possible to make changes in any organisation given time. Ask yourself how you could change your organisation by just one degree?

The Boss

I hate my boss

This is a pretty generic statement, so it helps to get under the skin of it. Why do you hate them? What do they do that you hate? If you don't find it easy to answer this, then think about how they make you feel. Then check out the excuse below that most closely applies.

My boss undermines me

It's no fun feeling undermined, is it? It can lead to feelings of frustration, misery and helplessness. The only way to tackle this is to take back some control so that you no longer feel helpless or frustrated. You may not be able to change your boss's behaviour - only they can do that – but you *can* change how you react to it, and you *may* able to influence how they react to you.

If they undermine you by taking credit for your work, make sure people know you did it. This could take the form of copying in others when you email your boss, or asking someone else to 'review' your work before it is passed to your boss (and then making sure your boss knows you have 'just run it past' someone else for their input or OK).

If your boss undermines you by criticising you in front of others you have two choices: fight back on the spot or take issue with them afterwards.

Fighting back in the moment isn't always the best solution because it's very hard to stay unemotional, but just occasionally it can be really powerful.

Take back some control so that you no longer feel helpless

Don't get sucked into defending yourself in front of others – that has the potential to spiral downwards into a slanging match or to end in tears. Tell them you'd prefer to have the conversation privately as you really don't think your colleagues want to be embarrassed/bored/delayed by listening to them give you feedback, and ask when would be a good time to meet to have that private discussion.

If you can't (or don't feel it's right to) fight back on the spot, try to stay as calm and unemotional as you can whilst it's happening. Silently remind yourself that the *way* your boss is giving feedback is as much about their inadequacies as a manager as it is about you. At the same time, listen hard for the truth in what they say.

There may be a small nugget of useful feedback hidden in the negativity!

Then make sure that you do take up the issue with your boss on a one to one basis as soon as you possibly can. Don't let it fester! Ask them for 5 minutes to follow up on their feedback. If you have managed to listen objectively to the feedback, acknowledge the issue they raised, thank them for the feedback, tell them that you found it embarrassing/upsetting to hear it in front of others, and tell them that you would prefer to have a private discussion next time.

Many of us shy away from talking about our emotions with our colleagues, and especially with our bosses. We fear they will think us weak and emotional. But they have emotions too! Usually it isn't hearing emotion described that makes our colleagues uncomfortable – it's witnessing emotion. So get all of your emotion out in private, at home, or with colleagues you like and trust to support you, and then put your objective hat on when you embark on the difficult conversation.

My boss treats me like a machine

If you're good at your job you will attract work, because

people know you will deliver. Sometimes you attract so much work that you can end up feeling like your boss thinks he is managing a factory. They can feed work into you at one end and receive it out the other!

What's happening is that you are not taking control. Unless you speak up when you get too much work, nobody will know until your work suffers and you end up letting colleagues down.

So for your own sake *and* for the sake of others, practice saying *No*. Don't get hung up on 'they'll think I'm no good' or 'they'll think I'm wimping out'. You're not. You *are* making sure that you continue to produce good quality work and that they don't inadvertently jeopardise that.

You may also like to take a look at *"Everyone delegates to me"* in the section on colleagues.

I don't trust the management

If you have evidence that the management is untrustworthy you have three choices:

- Collude with them
- Expose them
- Walk away

Only you can decide which of these you want to do.

Collusion may feel like the only option if you feel vulnerable, but it will probably make you miserable, uncomfortable and could ultimately land you in trouble if the lack of trust is serious. So be very sure that you have no alternative, or that it's worth it.

Exposure takes knowledge and courage. You need to gather facts or at least circumstantial evidence. You need to identify the right person to take this information to. Is there a whistle-blowing policy in your organisation? If so can you use it? If not, is there a colleague you trust with whom you can talk this over?

If you feel unable to collude or expose the truth, you really have no option but to plan your escape route. Advice on looking for another job or career is outside the scope of this book, but start by thinking about what you really want from your next job in terms of the values of the organisation, and the content of your work.

My boss is a bully

Being bullied in any environment is horrible – and unacceptable. Your ultimate recourse is to law, probably via a harassment claim. However, most of us don't want to go to that extreme until we've made other attempts to change the situation.

So I'd suggest the following steps:

• Get clear on whether you are genuinely being bullied

• Get clear on whether you are being singled out or whether the boss bullies others

• If it's just you (or mainly you) get clear on whether you are contributing to the problem

• Involve others in tackling the problem

First of all ask yourself whether an outsider observing your interactions with your boss would consider it bullying. It's hard to be objective, but try to separate how *you* feel about the way your boss behaves with what others would actually see.

What are the triggers for the behaviour that upsets you?

If it's not 100% clear that bullying is taking place, ask yourself what you could do differently to change the relationship with your boss. What are the triggers for the behaviour that upsets you? How can you avoid or at least minimise these triggers?

If you are clear that bullying is taking place, is it just happening to you? If so why do you think this is? What is there in your relationship with the boss that impels him or her to mistreat you? For what do you need to take responsibility? For what do they need to take responsibility?

Whether or not it's just you, now that you have gathered this information, it's time to take action. I suggest you start by trying to speak with the offender, to explain how you feel and ask for their help in changing the dynamic between you. If this is possible for you, that's great. They may not realise the impact of their behaviour on you, and it's good to give them an opportunity to change. If you can't speak to them, or if doing so gets you nowhere, it's time to involve others. You could talk to a trusted senior colleague, or if there's an HR department where you work, you can speak to them. You have every right to put a stop to this.

You may also like to read *"I'm being bullied"* in the section on colleagues.

My boss is a useless manager

Most people are not naturally great managers! Most of us have to work at it. How can you help your boss to be a better manager? Is there some specific feedback that you could give them? If so, be sure not just to tell them what you don't like, but also how you would prefer it to be handled.

Is there something you believe you could do better than them and if so, can you offer to help or take on that task/role?

Even if you aren't officially a manager in the organisation, we all have opportunities to manage – our own time, our children, a social event with our friends or colleagues, a project that involves others. Can you set a good example of management outside of your main role?

My boss makes me feel stupid

Actually your boss can't *make* you feel anything. We are all responsible for our own feelings – though of course it's very hard to stay strong when someone else is being hurtful.

Do they make you feel stupid because they criticise your work all the time? If so, is there any

We are all responsible for our own feelings

justification for this? What can you do to improve your work and/or demonstrate to them that you are really committed to getting better? Maybe it's asking for extra help, or offering to correct work in your own time, or asking for more training.

You may also want to read the advice for *"My boss undermines me"* earlier in this section.

My Team

I'm no good at managing people

It's not unusual for organisations to promote people into management positions without giving them any training. There seems to be an assumption that once you have a role, you automatically know what to do. And even if you have had some training, you may still need more before you feel confident that you have the management thing sussed. That's okay!

Start by getting clear on what you mean by saying you are 'no good' at managing people. For example: do you find it hard to tell others what to do? Do you find it difficult to explain things to others? Do you feel embarrassed because you are not confident that you have the right to be in charge of others?

There are a number of ways in which you could get help:

- you could read a book
- you could listen to a podcast
- you could observe or talk to other managers whom you respect

- you could ask your HR department what courses are available
- you could research courses to see what you would like to attend
- you could find yourself a mentor

Decide which of these sounds the most helpful, easy or relevant, and take action.

I don't like managing people

If not, why not? Is it because you don't feel confident? If so you may like to read the advice for the previous excuse above to find ways of building your confidence.

Also, don't be afraid to delegate the responsibility for managing some people, or some aspects of management, to another person who is good at this and enjoys it. It is not failure to share out the roles in your team so that you are playing to each person's strength.

I have nobody to delegate to

If you have lots of work and nobody to delegate to it

can be really stressful. Here the challenge is to push back when people are piling the work on and renegotiate either workload or timescale.

Think of each piece of work as sitting in a triangle where the three points are Quality, Time and Resource. Each piece of work needs a balance between the three, so if a really high-quality piece of work is needed, then sufficient time and resource must be allocated to it. Conversely if something is needed urgently then either the quality will suffer or more resource must be dedicated to it. Using this concept to clarify the priorities can be really useful both for you and when negotiating with those giving you the work.

My team is dysfunctional

You may have a mismatch of skills and strengths. By skills I mean what people can do and by strengths I mean how they do it.

Skills may be specific to the type of work you do – technical or intellectual expertise – or they may be specific to the role you have – e.g. project management, administrative, commercial, etc. Most teams have a good blend of skills, if not the perfect set, and you probably know what skills you need and whether you have them.

Strengths, on the other hand, are specific to the individual, and are more about their preferred style of working. Examples include:

Detail focused	Initiator
Visionary	Challenger
Facilitator	Peacemaker
Collaborator	Analyst
Completion-oriented	

Most of us combine two or more of these, and most of us *can* do other roles – but we all have a preference. Teams are at their most effective when we play to our strengths, have a good mix of styles *and* respect our differences. So how well do you know the strengths of your team, and what can you do to enable individuals to play to their strengths?

> Teams are at their most effective when we play to our strengths

I can't get my team to pull together

Many organisations skimp on team building and yet it is

a crucial element of a successful organisation. There are a number of ways that you can work on team building. Some of these are implicit and others are explicit.

It can be done within the business setting, by networking, sharing ideas and exploring each other's motivations. A good starting point is to ensure that there are opportunities for people to chat informally around work and other issues.

Or it can be addressed more explicitly, typically in an informal external setting, via a teambuilding event. These can take the form of activities designed to stretch you physically, mentally and/or emotionally, such as abseiling or role-playing exercises. Alternatively, you could work with a facilitator who will help you to address specific issues.

My Colleagues

I'm being bullied

Bullies are usually weak people who use fear to cover up their own feelings of inadequacy. Seeing them from this point of view can help to change your perspective and realise that the bullying is about his or her issues, not yours. I'm not suggesting that this makes it easy to cope with, but some people do find that it helps.

Is it just you they bully, or do they make a habit of it? If it's just you, then what is it about your demeanour or behaviour that encourages this response? How can you change your attitude to them to become more robust and less of a victim? For some people this is about pushing back the next time the bullying starts. For others, it's about identifying a supporter within the organisation who will reassure them that they don't deserve this treatment, and who will support them in tackling it.

You may also like to read *"My boss is a bully"* in the section on The Boss.

I feel isolated at work

You may feel isolated for a number of reasons. Perhaps you work from home, or in another environment where you don't see other people very often. If this is your issue, how can you find opportunities to meet up with others working in the same field – inside or outside your organisation? Is there an office you can visit from time to time, or more frequently than you do now? Are there internal events that you could make an effort to attend? Or events run for your industry - conferences, seminars or training – that you could sign up to?

Many of us find that we use email too much, and consequently fail to speak to or meet with others out of habit. Over time this means we have less human inter-action, which can lead to feelings of isolation. So next time you start to type an email to a colleague, **stop**! Pick up the phone, or if they work in the same building, go and see them instead.

If your reason for feeling isolated is one of not being 'part of the crowd' at work, what can you do to improve matters? Maybe there is someone else there with whom you feel you could have something in common. Start by building a rapport. Take an interest in who they are out-side of work. Ask them what they did at the weekend, or whether they had a good evening the night before. Once you have built some empathy, see if they would like to go for coffee, or lunch, and take time to get to know them better.

I don't like my colleagues

None of them? This is a sweeping statement – might it be because you feel bullied, or isolated? If so, see the advice in the first chapter in this section.

Or maybe the rest of the team seem to spend all their time talking about issues that don't interest you. Is there something which interests you that you could talk to them about?

It can be hard to raise this the first time, so rather than launching in with the whole group, identify the one or two team members whom you feel most comfortable with and find an opportunity to chat with them on a one to one basis. Start by asking them about their weekend or evening and make an effort to take an interest. Then, whether they ask or not, volunteer what you were doing and tell them what you enjoy about it.

See also *"I don't have any friends at work"* in the section covering issues with friends.

Everyone delegates to me

It's really tough when work is coming at you from all directions. The challenge here is to be assertive and take control, but don't make the mistake of confusing assertive with aggressive! Being assertive means you are being clear on what you stand for and you have the confidence in your right to claim that.

Be assertive and take control

So if for example you stand for high quality, well researched work, how can you deliver this consistently if you are forced to rush?

Try practising this: when asked to take on a new piece of work, don't immediately say yes. Pause, check in with yourself and your 'to do' list to see:

* Whether you want to do it
* When you could start it
* How much time you would need to do an excellent job
* Whether excellence is what is required, and if not what other approach you could adopt
* Whether someone else would be better placed to do it

Then armed with this knowledge, you can respond with:

- Yes, that's fine. I can get that back to you on.....
- I'm happy to take that on, and can we clarify the scope so I can let you know when I can do it
- I don't think I'm the right person to do this because... Have you thought of asking X who might be better than me because....

See also *"I have nobody to delegate to"* in the section dealing with your team.

I'm constantly distracted

If your colleagues frequently interrupt you then this will have become a habit – for them and you. So you need to break the habit and form a new one. Work out how you would like things to work, and then establish a new pattern to your working day.

Do they interrupt you to ask work-related questions, or to gossip?

If their questions are work-related, are they generally legitimate questions, and are you the right person to ask? If the answer is yes to both, then your task is to decide how often in the working day or week you are prepared to devote time to supporting your colleagues. Let them know that you want to support them but that you need to be more focused in your approach so the team as a whole can be more effective. Allocate specific times when you are 'open for business' for team support. Or if they are more senior than you, ask if you can agree a process for you to go to them once or twice a day or week to check on what they wish you to do.

Allocate specific times when you are 'open for business'

If they have work-related questions but shouldn't be asking you, you need to start pushing back. It's all too easy to be lazy and ask the most amenable colleague for help with everything, without either trying to think it through for yourself or identifying a more appropriate source of help. So if you get pestered with irrelevant work questions, redirect them to the right person – or tell them to have another go at figuring it out for themselves. Be persistent and they will eventually get the message.

If it's gossip that distracts you, speak up and say you are struggling to concentrate and that you'd love to catch up but at an agreed time, maybe over coffee or lunch. Don't get sucked in and don't heave heavy and meaningful sighs! If they must

Speak up and say you are struggling to concentrate

chatter (and assuming you have no authority to stop them yourself) keep politely reminding them that it's distracting you, and ask them to go somewhere else. As a last resort you can complain to a more senior colleague, but try to resolve it yourself first so as to preserve goodwill.

Recognition

Nobody values the work I do

It can be hard when you feel that those around you don't see the value you bring to the organisation. Do you think it is valuable? If not, you may want to read *"The work we do is meaningless"* in the Organisation section.

If *you* believe that what you do is valuable, make a list of the ways in which it adds value to the organisation and/or to society as a whole. Ask your friends, family, or a friendly colleague to help you come up with a list that is as long as you can make it. At this stage don't worry how accurate, sensible or business-like the list is – just jot everything down.

When you've done this, take a break, then sit back and read through your list again. You may find that this helps to reaffirm to yourself what value you bring, and that you now feel better and more confident in your role in the organisation. If that's all you needed, fantastic! But it's likely you also want others to recognise the value of your work. So you need to start thinking about how you can draw this to their attention.

Which items in your list are most likely to appeal to

your boss? Remember that the things that are important to you may not be the same. In most organisations the emphasis is on making money, and if this is true for yours, how does what you do add value in terms of helping the organisation to do just that?

If your organisation doesn't have the goal of making money, perhaps because it is in the public or caring sector, then focus on what the goal actually is, and think of your contribution in those terms.

Once you are clear how you add value to your particular organisation you have a choice in how you communicate it to others.

If you are feeling brave (or desperate!) you can take the direct route and ask your boss for a short meeting to discuss your role. At the meeting tell them honestly that you feel your work isn't valued and, drawing on the things you've identified, explain why you think it should be.

If you aren't ready for such a bold approach, watch for opportunities to talk about the value you add. This may require a change of attitude on your part. You cannot wait for others to notice what a good job you are doing (that clearly isn't working for you). So you have to tell them. This doesn't mean shouting about how great you are, but does mean telling others when you think something has gone well, or how pleased you are that you've achieved X. And it can mean volunteering to take on other work - not necessarily additional work-load, but speaking up when work is being allocated and indicating where you feel you can best contribute.

This approach may not bring instant results, but over time you should start to be recognised for what you do.

My boss never says thank you

Some of us need more thanks and appreciation than others. And there are many different leadership styles, some of which will suit you and some which won't. When you work for a boss whose leadership style does suit you, it's a pleasure to work for them, because you feel inspired, energised and motivated. When their style doesn't suit you, the opposite can be true.

Do you think you are treated differently from others in not being thanked? If so, then try to work out why. Does the way you work irritate your boss? Or doesn't your boss see the value in what you do?

If you aren't singled out for special treatment, because this is how the boss behaves with everyone, then either your boss doesn't see the need for thanks because it isn't how they themselves are motivated, or they lack leadership skills.

Either way, once you realise that this is about them and not you, it can ease the feelings of resentment. There is probably a limited amount you can do to change their behaviour, so apart from giving feedback when you get the opportunity, a more realistic approach will be to change how you respond. Look for other ways to get satisfaction – perhaps by working with colleagues to support and thank each other, or by simply taking pride in a job well done and knowing you've done your best.

My appraisal is always a disappointment

The best appraisal shouldn't contain any surprises. It should simply be an opportunity to consolidate feedback given/received over the year, and also a chance to discuss any action required to address weaknesses and to build on strengths.

However, the reality is that many of us have appraisals that fall short of this ideal. So what can you do to improve your chance of a satisfactory outcome to your appraisal?

First, gather your evidence:

- Review your goals or targets for the year and consider what you need to do to demonstrate your performance when measured against them
- If you need data to prove you have done a good job, make sure the data is available. A colleague of mine used to be one of our best salesmen, but he was very lazy about entering his sales into the organisation's database – so the data didn't support his claims of success!
- If you need feedback from colleagues, make sure it has been collected. Depending on your organisation's system, either remind colleagues of the work you have done together and ask them to provide feedback to your boss, or collect the evidence yourself. Ask for feedback and make a note of what they say, or better still ask them to email it to you and save those emails in a safe place
- If your organisation has a structured approach to appraisals, in terms of forms or other information that have to be submitted in advance, make sure these have been done on time. Your boss is a busy person, and is less interested than you are in your development. So make it easy for them to see what you have achieved

Second, take time before your appraisal to think about what you want to say to your boss. Ideally be prepared for a balanced discussion that looks at both positive and negative areas. Where do you feel there is a need for improvement, or something on which you'd like constructive feedback? What are the key things that you are most proud of?

Third, take a constructive attitude with you into the appraisal. Be prepared to have a proper conversation, and really listen to what your boss says, rather than just waiting for your turn to speak. Make sure that you respond to their comments as well as getting across what you believe has gone well.

Finally, if the outcome is still disappointing, ask your boss what you need to do differently to demonstrate to them that you are worthy of a more positive outcome next time around.

Sometimes appraisals are disappointing because they go hand in hand with a pay review that is less than you had hoped. If this is the case, find out whether the issue is your personal pay review or the organisation's budget for pay reviews across the board. There is no point arguing for more pay if the organisation isn't giving any pay rises at all this year (or only in certain circumstances whose criteria you don't meet).

Money

I'm not making as much money as I think I should

Are you being fairly paid for what you do? By that I mean would another person with your skills and experience earn a similar amount? If so, you are probably earning the going rate for what you do (and if not, see the next excuse below).

So then the question is, what is driving you to want more money? This is not as simple a question as it sounds. There are many different motivations for wanting money:

- The need to pay basic bills, so as to live without worrying about food, shelter and warmth
- The desire to provide for family, especially spouses and children at whatever level feels right for you
- The desire for some luxuries, or to indulge a personal passion (expensive car, owning a horse, foreign travel....)
- The desire for status and/or recognition
- The love of money for its own sake

If you need money so that you have enough to live on, that's one thing – and it's not only understandable, but a key component of how our society works. If you can't earn enough money from what you currently do, there are two routes to explore:

- Can you do some additional paid work elsewhere that will help to support you? This could be anything from a few hours a week working in a shop or bar, offering existing skills to friends or family for a fee, taking part in market research or surveys, etc
- Can you improve your value either to your current employer or to equip you to find other work that is better paid? This might involve studying, or asking for a mentor, or offering to take on projects outside the scope of your normal work to develop new skills

Ultimately, you may need to change jobs.

For some of us though, striving for more money is not about having enough to live on, or to pay for little luxuries. It's a habit. Our society is very money-oriented and people's success can be measured by their financial situation.

Work out what really matters to you

So if you feel like you are on a money-earning treadmill where you have to spin the wheels ever faster to earn more and more, it may be time to stop and think.

Take stock, and work out what really matters to you – more money, or time to spend with family and/ or friends, time to relax and engage in hobbies, time to explore and learn more about something that fascinates you?

My colleagues earn more than me

First of all, are you sure? In some organisations it's hard to know what others earn, and people can exaggerate! If you are sure, then it's time to dig a little deeper and find out why. Try to do this from an objective stand-point. I know this isn't always easy; money and fairness are very emotive topics. So if you can, ask for the opinion of a trusted friend, family member or colleague.

Look for the differences between those other people and you. These differences could relate to:

- The kind of work they do – do they have some skills that enable them to do work you can't?
- The way they do their work – do they behave in a way that makes them more effective, perhaps by relating well to customers, helping other colleagues,

or putting themselves out to deal with urgent issues outside standard working hours?

- The amount of work they do – are they quick workers, who get through their work more quickly than you do, thereby enabling them to do more in the day?

If you can't identify this, why not ask your boss? Most managers are happy to give constructive input to people who genuinely want to improve. So make sure you approach the conversation from that perspective, rather than from the perspective of complaining!

Once you know what separates you from your colleagues, you have two choices. You can accept that you earn less because you are less skilled, less effective with customers, slower, etc. or you can take action to close the gap between you.

If you want to take action, think about the steps you can take to move towards your goal. Can you gain more skills to make you more valuable to your organisation? Do you need help to manage relationships better? Do you need more practice at your current work so you can speed up? Depending on the type of improvement needed, there are a number of things you could try:

- Read a self-help book
- Go online and find a course you can do remotely
- Find a local college or other organisation that runs evening classes
- Ask your boss for more training or support
- Find a mentor who can guide you
- Volunteer somewhere that will help you develop new skills
- Put in extra time of your own to practice the things that need improving or speeding up (maybe it's something you can take home and work on there?)

If you genuinely can't identify the reason why your colleagues earn more than you, then it's just possible you are being discriminated against in some way. If you think this is the case, start by making some notes on why you think this is the case. You will need evidence to support your argument, so make sure you capture this as well. Sometimes writing everything down can help you to see things more clearly, too.

Your next step will be to talk to your HR department about it, if there is one. If not, you may be able to approach your boss with a request for them to hear your point of view. If you can't reach a satisfactory conclusion you may want to seek help from Citizen's Advice (online or in person at a local office).

I'm underpaid for the work I do

How do you know? If you believe that colleagues earn more than you, then go back to the excuse above. If you don't have colleagues with whom to compare yourself, what is it that indicates to you that you're underpaid? Is it the complexity of the work, or that it requires you to work in unpleasant conditions, or anti-social hours?

Assuming you're not self-employed, you need to put together an argument for better pay, so that you can talk to your boss. So gather your evidence. Think about the impact there would be on the organisation if you were to leave. How would they replace you and what would this cost them? Set out the skills you have that others don't, and the value this adds to the organisation.

Set out the skills you have that others don't

Ideally, talk your position through with an impartial friend. Ask them to look for the flaws in your argument, and then work out how to remove those flaws. If your friend says your argument is weak, listen to them! You may not like it, but it's better to hear it from them than from your boss. Think how you can strengthen your case, so that you have a better chance of being heard when you do go through official channels.

Confidence

I'm not up to the job

Whether you are telling yourself this, or hearing it from others, you need to change the story. There's a saying credited to Henry Ford (founder of the Ford Motor Company) that goes "whether you think you can or you think you can't, you're right".

Our brains are very complex, but they can be tricked. If we allow our brains to think we're a failure – we will fail. Conversely, there is plenty of evidence to show that when we tell our brains to focus on what we are good at, and keep reinforcing that message, we'll succeed.

A good way to start is by focusing on the things you do well. Every night before you go to bed, list three things you do well in your job and say them aloud (your brain needs to *hear* the words!) Then repeat them the next morning before you go to work. At any point during the day when your confidence wobbles, mentally hold up a 'STOP' sign in front of the negative thoughts, and repeat the positive ones to yourself again – out loud is best but silently will do.

Practise this every day, identifying a different list of three things you do well each day, and you'll soon find that you can shift into a more positive frame of mind whenever you need to.

You may also want to read *"I'm always worrying about work"* in Work/Life Balance.

I'm too disorganised

Some people are naturally organised, and others aren't. This is purely a personality trait, in the same way that some of us are extroverts and others introverts. So if you are not naturally organised, it is nothing to be embarrassed about or ashamed of. You will probably have other assets such as great creativity, artistic ability or the capacity to innovate rather than follow directions. Your ideal job will play to these strengths.

If you are not naturally organised, it is nothing to be embarrassed about

However, in most jobs being disorganised does mean that you will need to work a bit harder at certain things. Often the best approach is to sit down with a colleague who has organisation sussed, and ask for their help to identify:

- The tasks you have to do (non-negotiables)
- The tasks you could delegate, and to whom
- The tasks that are optional and which you could stop doing or do less frequently

Then get them to take a look at the tasks you have to do and suggest ways to do them more efficiently.

I keep expecting them to discover I'm a fraud

This is a really common fear. In fact it even has a name: 'Imposter Syndrome'. So you are absolutely not alone in feeling like this. It's really normal to imagine that someone is going to find you out, i.e. discover that you are not who you say you are.

You are absolutely not alone in feeling like this

However, there is a reason you have your job. It is rare these days to be handed jobs on a plate, so the chances are that you demonstrated the skills and/or experience required for the job when you were hired or before you were promoted.

Whilst really serious cases of imposter syndrome

may call for counselling, for most of us the best anti-
dote is just to get on with the job and prove to ourselves
(and, along the way, to others) that we have got what it
takes to do a great job.

Don't worry about making the occasional mistake;
we are not born knowing how to do everything and, like
babies who learn to walk by falling over a lot, you will
make progress so long as you learn from your mistakes.

I'm worried about losing my job

If you are worried about losing your job, then facing up
to the worst possible outcome can actually bring some
relief. If you lost your job, what's the worst that could
happen?

It can help to sit down and make a list of all the
consequences of losing your job. Getting them down in
writing may seem scary but it can also help to stop all
the worries going round and round in your head.

Once you have the list, try to take a step back and
look at it objectively. If you have a close friend or family
member with whom you can do this, fantastic. If you
don't feel able to do that (or not yet) then that's OK too.

Working through your list, there will almost certainly be things you can't control – the economy, the

financial state of the organisation (unless you are on the Board, in which case you may be able to have a significant impact), social changes that affect the success of your organisation. But what do you have on your list that you *can* control, even if only to a small extent?

If you're worried about getting into debt, what action can you take now to reduce your outgoings? Do you need help with managing your finances? Talk to your bank or mortgage provider now – they much prefer you to approach them before there's a crisis.

Are you worried about how others will react? Often our fear of this is much worse than the reality. So do please consider confiding in a close family member or friend. If you start by sharing your fears with just one person it can really help. If you dread telling your spouse or partner, don't beat yourself up. Sometimes it's easier to start by confiding in a friend or family member who is less close to you emotionally or who will be less affected by the consequences of you losing your job.

Are you worried about what you will do instead of this job? Before you jump in to job-hunting for a similar role, take time to assess what you would really like to do.

If you love the work you do, then seeking a similar job elsewhere may be the right approach. If not, think about what else you could do using your existing skills, or whether there's some training or studying you could start alongside your current job.

I keep making mistakes

When we make mistakes, it's disruptive. It disrupts the rhythm of our work, it disrupts our confidence in ourselves, and ultimately it disrupts our relationship with our employer. So if you are constantly making mistakes, it will be difficult to love your job. Something needs to change.

Before you can take action, ask yourself why you make mistakes. It could be any of the following reasons:

- you are being asked to do work for which you have insufficient training
- you are overtired or unwell and not thinking clearly
- you are nervous or scared and this is causing you to make mistakes
- you are working carelessly
- you have too much work and so are trying to get through it too quickly
- your work is too easy or monotonous and you are bored

Once you know the source of the problem it's easier to do something about it. If you have insufficient training you need to get some more – either by asking for a formal training course or by getting a colleague to show you what to do. If you are tired or unwell, you need to get help.

If you are nervous or scared then you need to tackle the cause of this as otherwise you'll continue to make silly mistakes. You may know what is making you nervous or scared, but if not, then reading through this book may help. If one or more excuses resonates with you, you will know there is something that needs to be addressed.

If you are overly tired, see *"I'm so tired that my work is suffering"* in the Health section.

If you are working carelessly because you see no meaning in your work, see *"The work we do is meaningless"* under The Work.

And if you're making mistakes because you have too much work, see *"I have too much work"* under The Work.

Personal Growth

I'm not learning anything

Some of us are perfectly happy to do the same work day after day, staying well within our comfort zone, and dealing with the tasks that are familiar to us. Others need the stimulus of learning something new – new information, new techniques, new skills.

Many if not most of us move between the two states. We are happy to consolidate existing knowledge and skills for a while, and then need new input to keep us interested and committed to our work.

If you are at a point in your job where you feel you are no longer learning anything – and that bothers you – then you need to take action:

- **Ask your boss** for more training, or more challenging work; maybe you can volunteer for projects that will stretch you or help a more experienced colleague with his or her work
- **Teach yourself** something new (from books, the internet, or an evening class)
- **Set yourself a challenge** to become even better at the job you currently do – fewer errors, faster

delivery, a higher take-up rate, more satisfied customers – whatever measure suits your role.

If none of these actions work, then it is probably time to acknowledge that you have outgrown this job, and it's time to move on.

I'm bored

If you are bored, ask yourself why.

If the work is too easy for you, see *"I'm not learning anything"* above

You might also find some useful advice in the section covering The Work - *"I don't like the work"*, *"I don't have enough work"* and *"I'm in a dead end job"*.

I'm not fulfilling my potential

During our careers, for most of us there are times when we progress really quickly and other times when it feels like we are standing still. This is normal – and desirable. It can be exhausting and stressful to keep progressing without any periods of consolidation. So take a good look at your job, look back at what you were doing at work five years, two years and one year ago and see whether you have made progress.

If you have indeed made progress, congratulations! Are you sure that you are not fulfilling your potential, or in the process of fulfilling it? Is it just that you need to continue to consolidate the skills you have developed before moving forward again?

If however this exercise simply proves what you feel instinctively, that you are not fulfilling your potential, then you need to take action. Nobody else will be as interested in your career as you are, so it's not only in your own interests, but also your responsibility to identify what is needed to help you fulfil that potential.

What can you suggest that will help you move forward?

Rather than complaining to your colleagues or to your boss, what can you suggest that will help you move forward? Imagine for a moment that your boss came to you and offered you the most exciting and challenging opportunity you can envisage. What would it be?

What are the elements that make it exciting and challenging? Is it the technical content? The skills you would need? The people you would deal with? The impact it could have on the organisation – or the world at large? The recognition it would grant you, inside or outside your own organisation?

As you answer these questions, you will be clarifying the kind of change you need in your job – whether that be development or deployment of technical skills, an opportunity to demonstrate interpersonal skills, or more recognition and status.

Once you know what you need, it's time to work out how to get it. You may want to ask your boss for help, or find a mentor inside or outside your organisation that will help you, or you may be able to identify a project or task that you can undertake that will demonstrate your abilities.

Travel

I hate my journey to work

The issue here is usually journey time or mode of transport.

If it's journey time you have two choices:

- Reduce the time spent travelling
- Make better use of the time spent travelling

One way to reduce time spent travelling is to change home or work location. Are either of these possible? If not you'll need to be more creative. Would travelling outside of the rush hour reduce the journey time? If so how can you achieve this, at least one day per week or fortnight?

Have you double checked that you are taking the fastest route to work? It's easy to get stuck in a routine and always do what you've always done, even after roads have been improved, bus routes changed and train timetables updated.

If you've done all you can to reduce the journey time, what would make the journey more enjoyable? If you travel on public transport, how do you use the time? Reading a good book, listening to music or an audio book, watching a podcast or film on your smartphone or tablet are typical options.

You could also use the time to learn – a new language perhaps, or study something that interests you. I know someone who is an expert on Greek mythology because he is interested in it and spends hours reading about it. Being so fascinated he becomes completely absorbed in his reading and totally unaware of his surroundings. Time passes far more quickly when you're engrossed in something.

Time passes far more quickly when you're engrossed in something

If that doesn't appeal, try people watching! Pick someone near you at the start of your journey and imagine the story of their day, or their life. You can choose how realistic or far-fetched your story is.

Or get to know the places you pass on your journey. Notice the unusual buildings, open spaces, landmarks, etc. And get curious about them.

Hate your journey because of the mode of transport? Sometimes this is made worse by travelling when it's busy, crowded and slow. Is there really no alternative? Can you start work earlier or later, or work a compressed week – 4 long days instead of 5? Don't assume this isn't an option until you have tested it.

Or could you change the mode of transport for some of your journey – walk part of the way instead of taking the bus, perhaps? Sometimes the sense of well-being and satisfaction you gain from this can make the effort involved worthwhile.

There's too much travelling in my job

Is this a function of the nature of the job, or the way you do it? Sometimes we get stuck in a pattern and assume that the only way to do something is the way we currently do it. So whatever you do, ask yourself whether there is any possible way that you could reduce the amount of travelling, whilst essentially doing the same job.

Even if travelling is a key element of your work, maybe there is a small change you could make that would reduce the impact of it on you by just 2%. If so, start here and make that change. Try it out, see how it works. Then, once it is an established part of your role, look for another 2% (see *"I don't like the work"* for more on this approach).

Here are some suggestions to kick start your thinking:

- Work from home once a month, fortnight or week
- Pick one meeting you would usually travel to and turn it into a virtual meeting – phone call, Skype or video conference
- Review your diary for the next month and identify one journey that you can cancel
- Plan meetings so that you do all your travelling together and have other days that are home or office based

What can you do for yourself to reduce the amount of travel you do?

Location

I hate working in an office

What is it about the office environment that you hate? Is it the constraint of having to travel to the same building and sit in the same place every day? Do you long to have more freedom?

Many people assume that there is no flexibility in their working arrangements, but a little lateral thinking and then some subtle negotiation can work wonders. Assuming you like the job content then how can you deliver what is needed without being cooped up in the office so much of the time?

Do you have to be in the office all day?

Can you work from home one day a week? Do you have to be in the office all day or could you spend part of the day working from a local café or hotel lounge? With modern technology there is so much scope to be creative.

Or is there a more outdoor or travel oriented role that you could apply for within the same organisation?

And when you do have to be in the office, how can you make it a nicer place to be in? First of all, take a look at your immediate surroundings. Is it scruffy and unloved? Are there notes on the walls or old papers that could be cleared away and replaced with pictures or photos? Can you listen to music while you work - or move around to different locations within the building? Could you swap desks with a colleague occasionally?

I hate working in a busy town

Is it the commute to and from work that you hate, or the feeling of being trapped when you arrive? Is there constant noise outside, or do you hate the hustle and bustle of crowds whenever you venture out? Do you loathe looking out of the window and seeing nothing but buildings and concrete?

When we dislike something, there's a natural tendency to focus on what offends us. So if you like your job and there's no other reason to make changes, you need to change your perspective! Try brainstorming all the things that are good about working where you do, maybe get some colleagues involved and challenge yourselves to come up with 20, 30, 50 things that are great about your location.

Aspects to explore include:

- Local facilities – shops, places to eat or buy take-away lunch, entertainments
- Transport – it's usually easier to get around in a busy town
- Proximity to others – friends, social activities
- Diversity – there's often a richer blend of cultures
- Hidden treasures – even in the busiest of towns, there's often a little green space where you can escape for some fresh air and tranquillity, or a library or other venue with a room where you can relax and have some quiet time.

Once you have a nice long list, identify what you can do to take advantage of these things. Task yourself with doing one thing each week to improve the quality of your working life.

I hate being in an open plan office

For many people, an open plan office is the only working environment they have ever known. Whether or not this is true for you, what do you dislike? The lack of privacy, the noise, an irritating neighbour, the lack of control over the temperature?

Firstly, is there any opportunity to change where you sit? Many of us complain about our seating position without making any attempt to move. So before you do anything else, check that you have fully explored this option. Have you talked to your boss or line manager about the issues that bother you?

Assuming you've tried this, and it hasn't yielded the desired result, it's time to get creative. Whilst you almost certainly can't build a wall around your desk, you may be able to give yourself the illusion of greater privacy and peace. Sometimes rearranging the layout of your seating area so you can face a different way (even if only when taking calls) can make a big difference. If there's scope to decorate your seating area, how can you make it feel more welcoming or tranquil? Maybe a few pictures or photos would help, or a cushion for your chair.

A large plant (real or artificial) can work wonders for screening off a nearby neighbour. If it's real and has some sunlight, it will have the added bonus of giving off some oxygen to enhance your working environment.

There may not be much you can do to address the temperature issue, but do make sure you have the means to cool down or warm up – a fan is key when you get hot (even a hand held, battery operated one can help) and a throw or extra sweater/cardigan in your drawer is a great standby for chillier times.

Finally, is there somewhere you can retreat to from time to time, either when you really need to concentrate or just for some peace? Sometimes there are quiet areas or spare offices that can be used on an ad hoc or pre-booked basis, so make sure you make the most of these.

I don't like being stuck in one place

What would you prefer? If you want the opportunity to travel, do you want to do this within the context of a job, or separately? How much travelling? To where? Some people may be happy just having the chance to work in different locations within the same part of the country, i.e. without staying away from home. Others will yearn to explore different countries and cultures, and to range all over the world. And others will fall somewhere in the middle of these two extremes.

So start by visualising what 'not stuck' would look like. It may be that this is a huge step from where you are now, or it could be that just a small change would make all the difference to you. Either way, get a clear picture of what the ideal outcome would be.

Now, how can you take one small step towards that

ideal situation? Come up with as many ideas as you can before you home in on one. Here are some suggestions to get you started:

- Use your lunch break to explore the facilities around your workplace – museums, galleries, independent stores, open spaces, churches, libraries, free events, music venues…
- Maximise the use of your free time to get out and about. For example, aim to spend a weekend every month away from home in a different part of the country
- Start planning your next holiday (if budget is an issue, perhaps you could volunteer somewhere, thereby getting free accommodation)
- Plan a mini-break – a long weekend spent somewhere different whether in this country or abroad
- Create a business case for changing how you work in your organisation, perhaps getting involved in a project that involves working across different locations
- Talk to your boss about visiting other locations in which your organisation operates from time to time
- Research opportunities for roles in your organisation that are less desk-based, or office-based
- Explore the options for a sabbatical
- Explore the scope for flexible working in your

organisation so that you can work one day a week from somewhere else – your home, a local café, another office

When you have a list, which of your ideas feels the most attractive, or perhaps just the easiest? How are you going to make a start on it?

Work/Life Balance

I'm working too many hours

Is this because your contract requires long hours or because you have so much work it doesn't fit within your normal working day? Or maybe you don't work particularly long hours, but nonetheless want to work fewer – perhaps because you have other commitments.

The action you need to take depends on whether or not you are paid for all the hours you do. If you are, then it's time to take a good hard look at the balance in your life between work, money and your family and friends.

If money is the issue, then ask yourself: 'if I worked fewer hours, and earned less money, could I find other ways to make my money go further?' Sometimes when we work long hours we spend more on travel, food (ready meals, take-aways and eating out instead of cooking at home), treats to make up for our absence, etc.

If money is not the issue do you work long hours simply because the type of work you do requires it, or could you negotiate to work fewer hours? Shorter days or one day off per fortnight, perhaps?

If you're not paid for all the hours you do, then why are you working so hard? What is your motivation? Get clear on this first, because it will affect how you tackle the issue. Is it:

- Fear - 'if I don't put in all these extra hours I'll lose my job'?
- Peer pressure - 'everyone else works long hours so I have to too'?
- Conscience - 'in my role it's expected that I work long hours', or 'it's my responsibility to do a good job however many hours it takes'?

If it's fear, are you really sure that working fewer hours could jeopardise your job? If it could, then you need to address this - see The Work and My Team sections for advice on managing and reducing a heavy workload.

What can you do to maximise your efficiency?

If it's peer pressure, focus on output rather than input. Some of us work more efficiently than others, so can you achieve the same amount of work as your colleagues, but in a shorter day?

What can you do to maximise your efficiency? I would counsel against working through your lunch hour or without any breaks for tea/coffee. Research shows that we are actually much more effective and achieve more when we take regular breaks.

And when you have maximised your efficiency, make sure that others know about it! Don't let them upset you with snide remarks about part-timers when you leave at the end of the contractual day. Turn the tables on them and say you are sorry if they aren't capable of doing their work in the allotted time, or don't have a life outside work, but you are and you do!

If your conscience keeps you at work, then ask yourself if this is letting you down in other ways. What about your family? Are they getting a fair deal? What about your health? Are you taking care of that so it doesn't deteriorate and cause an even bigger problem at work?

I feel like I'm on a treadmill

If this is a temporary state of affairs, or has only happened recently, what has triggered it? There must be some reason why things have changed and you need to work out what this is.

Has a big order come in, which requires everyone to put in extra effort? If so, this can be a great opportunity for the team to pull together and bond in a new way.

How can you help to get the team fired up to see this as a challenge and a chance to do things differently? Whether you are a junior member or the team leader, you can play a part in this.

Have you got a new boss who drives everyone harder than their predecessor? They may be trying to prove themselves or have a remit to increase productivity. Sometimes the simplest action is the best: talk to them! Tell them how you are feeling and how things have changed since they arrived, and ask them what their strategy is. You might also ask them to share this with the whole team, as you probably won't be the only one feeling pressurised. Ask them what you can do to support them. This may feel scary but I promise you that most bosses welcome this kind of constructive questioning.

If work *always* feels like a treadmill, then you may not need help to love your job, you may need help to change it! So it's time to start exploring other roles, other companies/organisations or other careers. But before you do that turn to *"My boss treats me like a machine"* under The Boss.

I have no time to do the things I enjoy

It is a cliché, but no less true, that work expands to fill the time available. It's also true that we can get so used to spending all our time on work that we gradually let other activities slip.

Commit to re-introducing what you enjoy back into your life. First of all make a list of what you would like to do if you had more time. Make this list as long as you can. What did you do one, five or ten years ago that you don't do now? Try to come up with at least 20 things. Think about hobbies - things you'd do alone, those you'd do with friends and those you'd do with your family. Only you will see this list, so don't be shy to add things that seem frivolous or geeky.

Work expands to fill the time available

You will probably have some activities that only require a little time and others that need longer. So the next step is to divide your list up into those things that only take an hour or so, and those that require more time.

Now, take a good look at the 'quick to do' list and pick out one thing that you'd like to do in the coming next week. Then get out your calendar and book yourself a one-hour appointment to do it.

Then take a good look at the 'takes longer' list and again, pick out one thing you'd like to focus on. Get your calendar and work out when, in the next month, you could do it or make a start on it.

Tell a friend or family member that you are going to do these things, and ask them to hold you accountable for doing them. This will make it far more likely that you will do it. Maybe they would like to go through the same exercise, so that you can swap commitments and accountabilities. Or perhaps it's an activity that you can do together.

At the end of the month, check in with each other. How did you get on? If things went well do the same thing for the next month – book one quick to do and one 'takes longer' activity into your calendar. If things didn't quite go according to plan, identify what got on the way and take constructive action to clear the road-block. Maybe you picked the wrong time, or you didn't *really* put the time aside in your head as well as in your calendar. What will help you to have more success next month?

Like anything else, finding time to do the activities we enjoy needs practice to become a habit. Remember that you are a much healthier, nicer and more effective person when you have some downtime.

I'm constantly checking emails from home

Technology is both the boon and the bane of our modern lives. From a work perspective it enables us to stay in touch when we are on the move and it has made flexible working far more practical, with working from home (or a café, airport lounge, hotel room or even a beach) a real option.

The downside, of course, is that most of us no longer stop working when we leave the office. The temptation, and perhaps the expectation, is too great. So we continue to check our emails after we've finished our official working day.

For some of us this works fine. It enables us to keep an eye on what is going on, but not to get actively involved unless there is a real need. But some of us check our emails ever more frequently and never switch off. This can lead to stress and insomnia, and arguments with your nearest and dearest, who naturally get fed up at taking second place to your work.

The starting point for changing this is to know what you *need* to do to satisfy the demands of your job. Have you got into the habit of being available 24/7? That's not healthy for you or for your colleagues. You need downtime in order to be able to function at your best at work – never mind having a life outside work! So be clear what is expected of you in your job and push back if that assumes non-stop availability.

If you are very senior, and there is a real possibility of your input being needed at any moment, then find an alternative to constantly checking in. When I managed a department I had an agreement with my PA that when I was on holiday she would text me if there was an email I really needed to look at. Otherwise she knew (and anyone who asked her knew) that I would review my emails once a day and deal with anything that couldn't wait till my return.

> You need downtime in order to be able to function at your best

Once you have sorted out what is expected of you, the next step is to decide how you are going to meet that requirement. For example, if you are expected to check emails between 8am and 8pm, that doesn't mean you have to have your smart phone constantly buzzing every time an email comes in! If you were on a call, or in a meeting you wouldn't be expected to drop everything to deal with an email – in fact that would be downright rude as it suggests the person sending the email is more important than the person you are speaking to! So start to acclimatise yourself to a changed approach. I suggest you turn off alerts and start to wean yourself off your email checking habit by gradually increasing the intervals between checking them. For example, if you currently jump into action every time your phone buzzes, you may need to look at your emails every 10 minutes initially. Do this for the first day, then increase the intervals to 20 minutes the next day, and so on until you have reached your target.

In most organisations and for most roles, every half hour would be more than adequate during the working day, and every hour at other times – or you may be able to move to once or twice a day on non-working days.

I never see my family

There could be a few reasons for this:

- Does your job require a lot of travelling?
- Do you have to work and stay away from home for days or weeks at a time?
- Does your job require very long hours in the office or other working environment?
- Do you have a long commute?

Jobs that require a lot of travelling and/or staying away from home can be tremendous fun when you're young and single, but sometimes less fulfilling when they take you away from partners and/or children. If you've reached the point in your life where the fun has gone, maybe it's time to think about making a change. It's good to start by seeing how creative you can be about this.

Is there a way of getting your family to come and spend time with you rather than the other way round? One person I know flies out to join his wife every weekend when she is away on business projects – and often spends a long weekend with her, working remotely from her rented flat. This may be harder with school-age children, but there are always school holidays.

If that option isn't for you, is there anything you can do to reduce the amount of travelling whilst staying in the same role? We sometimes fall into the trap of thinking that there is only one way of doing things – and some organisations are more prone than others to think along traditional or conventional lines. How can you use technology to help you work more flexibly?

Working more flexibly may also help if you work long hours or have a long commute. The number of jobs where it is critical to be on site every day is reducing all the time as people recognise that it is perfectly possible to do a good job wherever you are, provided the internet and associated support are available. Lots of organisations have virtual teams where it is the norm not to sit alongside your peers or those you manage. So if you currently commute every day, can you negotiate to work **How can you use technology to help you?** one day a week, or even one day a fortnight, from home? Make sure you put together the business case for this – what's in it for the organisation, how you will handle the need for meetings, how you will set yourself up to be available and efficient.

If it's really impossible to change the way you do your role, it may be time to make a change. Could you change your role within the same organisation without jeopardising what you are good at and what you enjoy doing? Only when you have explored all the options to improve the balance between work and home where you are, should you think about the more radical step of changing jobs.

I'm always worrying about work

When you're constantly worrying you can't switch off and it's very hard to enjoy your so-called down time.

This can affect your sleep, and when you're sleep deprived everything seems harder, and problems seem bigger, which will lead you into worrying more. It's a vicious circle.

So how do you tackle this vicious circle? Firstly, get clear on what you are worrying about:

* Are you worried about making mistakes?
* Are you worried about letting others down?
* Are you worried about letting yourself down, due to not performing at your best?
* Are you worried about losing your job?

If you said yes to more than one of these, start by identifying the one that bothers you most. Tackle that first and then if necessary come back to the next one on your list.

Worried about mistakes? Take a look at *"I keep making mistakes"* in the Confidence section.

Worried about letting yourself or others down? This fear is often bound up with a feeling of responsibility or duty. It can help to remember that you are only responsible for doing your best, not for being superhuman. Doing your best includes making sure you have had the right training, whether that's on the technical content of the job or the softer skills that help you interact effectively with others.

Doing your best can also mean asking for help, either in the form of practical input or moral support. Depending on the nature of your job this could be a buddy, a mentor, a sponsor or a coach.

Worried about losing your job? Take a look at *"I'm worried about losing my job"* in the Confidence section.

I dread Mondays

Some of us actually quite enjoy our work during the week, but find that at the weekend (or our equivalent time off) we start to build up a picture of work that makes us anxious. That anxiety then builds as the working week approaches. If this is you then it's time to take control and work out what's going on.

Next weekend, or on your time off, keep a diary of your feelings. Whenever you notice the feeling of dread grab you, make a note. How does it show up? What are you doing at the time? What are the words that spring to mind to describe it? Does anything make it go away, or get worse? Adopt a spirit of curiosity rather than one of judgement.

Then it's a good idea to wait until you are in the middle of your working week before you revisit the issue. Whilst you are in the thick of work, check in with yourself to be sure that the feeling of dread isn't present. If it is, then you'll know this isn't just about dreading Mondays, but about more general work worries. Take a look at the advice for the other excuses earlier in this section.

If you're feeling OK mid-working week, get out your notes and look back at how you felt during your time off. Can you see a disconnect between then and now? What's the trigger that makes work scary when you aren't doing it? Once you can see this, you'll be in a better position to tackle it.

Friends

My friends all have better jobs than me

Many of us exaggerate the importance, prestige and interest in our jobs when we speak to others. So before you beat yourself up, are you sure this isn't a case of 'the grass is always greener on the other side of the fence'? Would you really want your friend's job – including the tedious, difficult or uninteresting aspects that they may not mention? Would it play to your skills and strengths? Would it be more enjoyable and satisfying than your own job, not just tomorrow, but in three, six, twelve months' time?

Is it money which causes you to classify your friends' jobs as 'better'? If so, are you sure that your understanding of what they earn is accurate? Before you jump into salary envy, are you certain that it is justified? Remember that when people appear to be affluent, and to spend money freely, that money could just as easily be money they have borrowed from the bank as money they have earned. Many people live a life weighed down with debts – and that is definitely not to be envied.

If after taking a long hard look at these questions, your answer is yes, then maybe there is something you need to do to explore how to love your current job more by finding ways to make it more interesting, fulfilling and financially rewarding. It is always better to take an active role rather than a passive one, so think how you can add skills or experience to enhance your value to your current organisation.

Or if you feel that your prospects are genuinely limited where you currently work, what can you do to prepare for your next job?

My friends make fun of my job

Let's draw a distinction between friendly teasing and unkind comments that upset you.

Most of us tease our friends from time to time – so if your friends are making fun of your job that may just be one way of them showing their affection for you. Or they may be hiding the fact that they secretly admire or envy what you do. If you have this kind of relationship with them, then no doubt you also tease them from time to time.

If you recognise this kind of relationship, but still dislike the teasing, there is probably something underlying your discomfort. Maybe you are also secretly unsure about the value of your job, and can actually understand why your friends comment as they do. If this is the case, look for more meaning in your work – see *"The work we do is meaningless"* in the first section of this book.

However, if the comments you receive are hurtful, unkind or cruel you have two choices. Explain to your friends how their comments upset you and ask them to stop, or decide that these so-called friends are not wanted in your life, and break away from them.

I don't have any friends at work

Some people are lucky, and find like-minded people at work who become friends as well as colleagues. For the rest of us, it's not that unusual to realise that we don't really have much in common with our colleagues, and that we certainly wouldn't describe them as friends.

There is no rule that says you have to make friends at work

So if this is your situation, first of all be aware that it

is completely normal. There is no rule that says you have to make friends at work, and particularly for those of us in a small team, or in a senior position, or who are very different in age to the majority of our colleagues, it's quite possible that we won't have enough in common to become friends.

It is however important that we get on with our colleagues well enough to work effectively with them. So even if you feel you have very little in common with them, take an interest in their lives. Find out what makes them tick, what family they have, how they like to spend their free time.

You could be surprised how much they appreciate you taking an interest in their lives, and how that enables you to form a closer relationship with them than you might have imagined possible. And don't forget to reciprocate. If they ask about your life outside work, share with them the things that you are happy for them to know.

See also *"I don't like my colleagues"* in the My Colleagues section.

Health

My job is too stressful

Your health is more important than anything else, so if your work is causing you significant stress something needs to change. The action you need to take will depend on the cause of your stress. If you already know exactly what is causing your stress, great, you're off to a good start.

If not, it may be useful to keep a diary for a week or so, making a note each time you feel particularly under pressure, upset, angry, or stressed in some other way. Write down what you are doing or have just done and how you feel. At the end of the week sit down and review the diary to see if you can identify a pattern of the triggers.

Once you know what is causing your stress, you need to identify what needs to change to stop it. At this stage assume that anything is possible; don't start seeing difficulties. For example, if your boss's manner towards you is upsetting, recognise it. Think how you would like them to behave towards you instead. If you have too much work, think how much work you could cope with without being stressed, and ideally think about how you would like your extra work to be handled – by another colleague, by turning away work from the organisation, by hiring extra resource or by streamlining activity to make it more efficient.

It is always better to identify possible solutions than to simply complain about what is wrong. Armed with this information the next step is to work out whom you should speak to. This may be your boss, or if they are part of the problem, it could be a peer, a senior colleague at the same level as your boss, someone even more senior or someone in your HR department (if there is one).

I faced this issue once when I felt there were serious issues with my boss, so I know just how difficult it can be to tackle it. I chose to ask the CEO for a meeting at which I laid out my concerns. He took time to listen, ask questions and to thank me for my input. I believe he also spoke to other colleagues in my team, some of whom raised similar issues. A few weeks later, changes were made which addressed my concerns. So raising your concerns can make a real difference.

I'm at breaking point

If you're under unbearable pressure, and assuming you're not self-employed, remember that your employer has a duty of care to its staff. So if work pressures are taking you to breaking point, that's another way of saying that it is affecting your health.

You have every right to complain, and to ask them to make changes, before you end up going off sick (and causing your employer an even bigger headache). It's not a sign of weakness to say 'enough!' It's a sign of a mature adult taking responsibility for his or her own welfare and ultimately acting in the employer's best interest.

I never get time for exercise

I believe there is *always* time to do *something*. You may not be able to take exercise in the form that you would ideally choose but you can find time to do *some* exercise.

For example, it might be difficult to find half a day to play a round of golf, or to play football with a local team, or to run a marathon. However, you can probably leave for work 10 minutes earlier and get off the train, tube or bus one stop before your usual one, so as to walk the rest of the way. Or go out at lunchtime and walk or jog around the block, or head to the nearest green space and run or walk around that.

If you can't get outside then endeavour to walk up and down stairs wherever you go (station, office, shops, home) instead of using the escalator or lift. If that's too easy, then run up and down whenever you can (without endangering others!) Use an app on your smartphone or buy a pedometer and monitor your steps each day.

Start with a small step, a simple adjustment to your week, to fit in just 30 minutes of exercise. This doesn't have to be all at once – walking one stop to the office three times a week may achieve it.

However if exercise is a passion and you want to fit in gym sessions, training for a 10k, dance classes, or whatever you love doing, take a look at *"I have no time to do the things I enjoy"* in the Work/Life Balance section.

Also, for more help with motivation to exercise you may like one of the other books in this series: *"What's Your Excuse for not Getting Fit?"*

I'm so tired that my work is suffering

What's causing your tiredness? Is it domestic (relationship issues, baby or young child not sleeping, caring for a sick relative, financial worries, etc) or work-related?

Either way you need to take some action.

If a domestic problem is making you tired, it is still worth having a quiet word with your boss or someone in HR to explain the situation, tell them you are addressing it and ask for their support and forbearance whilst you do so. Most employers much prefer to be alerted honestly to this than to find out only when things go wrong.

Clearly you do also need to address the issue. When we are exhausted our judgement can be impaired. It's really common to try to soldier on without asking for help, but help is what you need. If there's another family member who could help, get them involved. If the issue needs external help, ask for it. Your GP or the Citizen's Advice Bureau are two possible sources to get you started.

It is not acceptable for work to make you ill

If the problem is work-related then you definitely need to speak to your boss or someone in HR to discuss the issue. Remember that you have both the right *and* a duty to let them know what's going on. It is not acceptable for work to make you ill, and excessive tiredness can be a first step to illness.

If you can, be clear on what you would like to be different. Is it different working hours, or less work, or more support? Ideally have some suggestions about changes that could help you rather than simply a general complaint about what's not working well. Even if these changes aren't practical for the organisation, it will give them (and you) a starting point from which to explore options.

See also *"I'm at breaking point"* above and *"I have too much work"* in The Work.

Some Final Thoughts

I hope this book has helped you to identify ways in which you can get more enjoyment, satisfaction and even fun from your job.

If you are still hesitating over how to take action, here are some simple steps to get you started:

Maximise your motivation

Ask yourself: on a scale of 1 to 10, how much do I love my job?

If the answer to this isn't 10, then ask yourself, what would a 10 look and feel like?

Spend time imaging what would be different – how much better life would be, not just during the working day but outside it too. Think of the impact on your happiness, your health, your relationships with family and friends and your love life. Refer back to the benefits you listed at the start of this book.

Clarify what matters to you

What are your values, the things that really matter to you? No two people value exactly the same things, but to get you started, here are some examples of values that many people have:

Honesty	Loyalty
Family	Healthy living
Financial security	Integrity
Adventure	Faith

Nature/outdoors	Sustainability
Fun	Competition
Challenge	Connection
Variety	Giving back

If you find it hard to identify these, it is sometimes easier to spot when something you value is being compromised. Next time you get cross or upset, notice what it is that is having that impact. For example, if you get poor service in a shop and that annoys you, what is it that bothers you most? Is it the inefficiency, the bad manners, the waste of your time? These will imply that you have a value of efficiency or accuracy, courtesy or thoughtfulness.

Understanding your own values is a great foundation on which to build a plan of action.

Know what you are good at

What are your skills and strengths?

It may be quite easy for you to articulate your technical skills – knowledge you have by virtue of your education and subsequent training. So make a list of these. Think as widely as you can and capture skills you may have developed along the way, like IT skills or knowledge of how certain types of organisation tick.

It may be harder for you to identify your soft skills and your strengths. A good way to do this is to ask your friends and family to each name your five top qualities. You may be surprised at the consistency in their replies, or you may have a wealth of different views, in which case think about how you show a different side of your character in different situations.

Identify your goal

Armed with this information on what matters to you and what you are good at, think about the elements that you would love your job to contain.

This may relate to one of your values, such as more scope to make a difference in the world, more opportunity to spend time outdoors, or more financial reward. It may be about utilising a strength you have identified, such as solving complicated puzzles, making others feel good about themselves or having more time to spend with your family or friends.

Plan your action

Now you know what you want in your job, use this book, and your own ingenuity, to work out how to get more of this from your current job. You may be able to take some simple steps to improve matters in the short term, or it may be a case of taking some time to learn new skills, prove your worth to the boss or research other roles.

Go for it!

No more procrastinating! It's time to put your plan into action. If this feels daunting, enlist the support of a friend to encourage you and hold you accountable for taking action. Maybe they could also get more enjoyment from their job, and you can support each other. Don't get disheartened if your first attempt fails. It can take time and persistence to get what you want. Remind yourself that it will be worth it. You deserve to love your job!

And if you need to move on....

If after reading this book you realise that you're never going to love your current job, it's time to move on. I encourage you to explore your options widely. Think about what is important to you. Understand your strengths. Have the courage to think beyond your current skills, and identify ways to acquire new skills to support a change of direction if that's what you want. Much of the advice on the previous few pages is still relevant to career changers.

Don't be afraid to seek advice or work with an executive coach. I know from personal experience as both client and coach just how helpful this can be. I would never have been so successful in my own career without the support of a coach, and I have seen many of my own clients go from strength to strength.

If this book has helped you I'd love to hear from you, or if you have an excuse that I have missed!
Email me at amanda@coachingwithamanda.com.

About the Author

Amanda Cullen is a coach who works with individuals and teams.

Before becoming a coach Amanda spent many years as a consultant at the human resources consulting firm Mercer, including 10 years as a partner. During that time she managed major accounts, led large teams and provided governance advice to pension scheme trustee boards.

She now helps individuals to step up to their full potential and to make the most of their roles, and she helps managers to become better leaders.

When working with teams Amanda increases their effectiveness by helping them to better understand each other's skills, strengths, styles of working and motivations. She also specialises in board effectiveness work.

Amanda lives in Surrey but has helped individuals and teams from all around the world.

Acknowledgements

I undertook my coaching training with the Coaches Training Institute and later with CRR Global, and the influence of their teaching runs throughout this book. Most of my career was spent with the consulting firm Mercer, where I was fortunate to experience a wide range of formal and informal development, and to benefit from some excellent bosses and mentors.

I'd like to thank Joanne Henson for being the inspiration behind this book.

I have learned a lot from my coaching clients, who have brought a wide range of work-related issues to me. These have been in my mind as I wrote this book.

Index

Also in this series

What's Your Excuse for not Eating Healthily?

Joanne Henson
Overcome your excuses and eat well to look good and feel great

Do you wish you could eat more healthily and improve the way you look and feel, but find that all too often life gets in the way? Do you regularly embark on healthy eating plans or diets but find that you just can't stick with them? Then this is the book for you.

This isn't another diet book. Instead it's a look at the things which have tripped you up in the past and offers advice, ideas and inspiration to help you overcome those things this time around.

No willpower? Hate healthy food? Got no time to cook? Crave sugary snacks? Overcome all of these excuses and many more. Change your eating habits and relationship with food *for good*.

"Very useful, very practical and makes a lot of sense!

There are some great tips in here and even if you just implemented a bit of Joanne's advice it would make a real difference"

Paperback - ISBN 978-0-9933388-2-3
e-book – ISBN 978-0-9933388-3-0

Also in this series

What's Your Excuse for not Living a Life You Love?

Monica Castenetto
Overcome your excuses and lead a happier, more fulfilling life

Are you stuck in a life you don't love? Have you reached a point where your life doesn't feel right for you any-more? Then this book is for you.

This is not yet another self-help book claiming to re-veal the secret to permanent happiness. Instead, it helps you to tackle the things which have been holding you back and gives ideas, advice and inspiration to help you move on to a better life.

Don't know what you want? Scared of failure? Hate change? Worried about what others might think? This book will help you overcome all of your excuses and give you the motivation you need to change your life.

"Monica has a reassuring and wise voice throughout and gives you a sense of being in safe hands. Leave

those excuses on the shelf along with your unwanted fears and unfulfilled dreams"

Carole Ann Rice, life coach, author and columnist

Paperback – ISBN 978-0-9933388-4-7
e-book – ISBN 978-0-9933388-5-4

Also in this series

What's Your Excuse for not Getting Fit?

Joanne Henson
Overcome your excuses and get active, healthy and happy

Do you want to be fit, lean and healthy, but find that all too often life gets in the way? Do you own a gym membership you don't use, or take up running every January only to give up in February? Then this is the book for you.

This is not yet another get-fit-quick program. It's a look at the things which have prevented you in the past from becoming the fit, active person you've always wanted to be, and a source of advice, inspiration and ideas to help you overcome those things this time around. Change your habits and attitude to exercise for good.

Too tired? Lacking motivation? Bored by exercise? You won't be after reading this book!

"Joanne is a true inspiration! Her passion, commitment

*and no nonsense attitude never fails to motivate her
clients to get moving and achieve their health and
fitness goals"*

Sarah Price, triathlete and five times Ironman finisher

Paperback – ISBN 978-0-9933388-0-9
e-book – ISBN 978-0-9933388-1-6